Accelerated Reader
Level 5.6

HANG GLIDING

HEIDI ZEIGLER

HIGH
interest
books

Children's Press®
A Division of Scholastic Inc.
New York / Toronto / London / Auckland / Sydney
Mexico City / New Delhi / Hong Kong
Danbury, Connecticut

Book Design: Michael DeLisio
Contributing Editor: Matthew Pitt
Photo Credits: Cover © Chris Speedie/Getty Images; p. 3 © Digital Vision;
p. 5 © Galen Rowell/Corbis; p. 6 © Historical Picture Archive/Corbis;
pp. 8, 36 © Hulton-Deutsch Collection/Corbis; p. 11 © Bill Ross/Corbis; p. 13
© Jonathan Blair/Corbis; p. 14 © Kevin Fleming/Corbis; pp. 17, 27 © Morton
Beebe/Corbis; p. 18 © Vince Streano/Corbis; p. 21 © David Richardson/Index
Stock Imagery, Inc.; pp. 22-23 © Marck Hunt/Index Stock Imagery, Inc.; pp. 24,
40–41 © Omni Photo Communications/Index Stock Imagery, Inc.; pp. 30–31, 39
© Paul Gallaher/Index Stock Imagery, Inc.; p. 33 © Diaphor Agency/Index Stock
Imagery, Inc.; p. 34 © Bob Burch/Index Stock Imagery, Inc.; back cover
© Duomo/Corbis

Library of Congress Cataloging-in-Publication Data
Zeigler, Heidi.
Hang gliding / Heidi Zeigler.
    v. cm. -- (X-treme outdoors)
    Summary: Introduces the sport of hang gliding, including the techniques,
gear, and training needed, and touches on hang gliding competitions and
top competitors.
    Includes bibliographical references and index.
    ISBN 0-516-24320-9 (lib. bdg.) -- ISBN 0-516-24382-9 (pbk.)
    1. Hang gliding--Juvenile literature. [1. Hang gliding.] I. Title.
II. Series.

GV764 .Z45 2003
797.5'5--dc21
                                                        2002009170

CONTENTS

INTRODUCTION

The wind finally seems right. You take a few short running steps and launch off the hill into nothing but sky. The hillside slips away below you. Rather than falling, though, you begin to soar even higher! Your amazing power to "fly" comes from the nylon-covered, aluminum wing to which you're clinging—your hang glider.

You shift your weight and turn your wing to find thermals, or columns of warm air, that will carry you even higher. You ride these thermals thousands of feet above Earth. From here, you look down on the rolling hills and treetops beneath you. You are flying so high that even some birds are below you! High winds zip across your cheeks. The air is becoming colder the farther you climb into the sky. You wish you could stay aloft forever. Eventually, though, the thermals die down. It's time to dive back down. You carefully guide your craft in for a smooth landing. The moment you touch solid ground, you want to take off again. You can't wait for your next chance to soar.

An *X-treme* sport such as hang gliding can really change the way you view the world.

Hundreds of hang glider pilots admit that after their first experience in the sky, they were hooked on the sport. What other thrill can compare with such a mix of excitement, challenge, and freedom? This book will reveal how the dream of flying became the *X-treme* sport of hang gliding. You'll even learn how you can experience this amazing sport yourself.

CHAPTER ONE

SOARING TO NEW HEIGHTS

Men and women have dreamed of flying since they first gazed at the heavens thousands of years ago. They wrote myths and fables about people having the ability to fly like birds. One famous Greek myth involves a boy named Icarus. Icarus' father gives him wings made of wax. He warns his son not to fly too close to the sun. As Icarus flies, however, he grows arrogant and careless. He disobeys his father's advice. When Icarus flies too high, the sun melts his wings. He falls into the sea and drowns.

Throughout the ages, many great thinkers did more than compose fables about flight. Isaac Newton and Leonardo da Vinci spent countless hours trying to understand how birds fly. They drew sketches and studied the laws of physics to understand the

Ancient tales touch upon humankind's desire to reach the heavens.

Scientists have spent centuries trying to learn the mysteries of flight that allow birds to fly.

mechanics of flight. For the most part, however, the dream to fly remained grounded.

UP, UP, AND AWAY

In the late nineteenth century, a German named Otto Lilienthal made his dream of flying take flight. Despite the comments of critics, Lilienthal designed an early hang glider. Lilienthal built a wing made from wood and fabric. This wing connected to a curved wooden frame below it. Lilienthal climbed inside this wooden frame. Once inside the frame, he ran onto a springboard and leaped off. Once aloft, Lilienthal shifted his body back and forth to steer.

Lilienthal wanted to try more daring flights, but he faced a problem. The city he lived in, Berlin, Germany, was on flat land. However, Lilienthal did not let that stop him from using his device: he simply built a hill outside of the city! Lilienthal launched from the hill, then glided along the wind currents.

Lilienthal's breakthroughs soon inspired Orville and Wilbur Wright, who had their own dreams of flying. The Wright Brothers studied Lilienthal's work. Using some of his designs, they developed the first airplane. Their famous flight at Kitty Hawk, North Carolina, in 1903, was an astounding achievement. The high-flying success of the airplane made most people

X-FACTOR

Experts believe that a hang glider was the first spy plane! Over 3,000 years ago, Chinese soldiers were tied to gigantic kites. As they rose into the sky, these soldiers scanned the land for enemies.

forget about hang gliding. After all, why use your own energy to fly when you could use an airplane with an engine instead?

A scientist named Francis Rogallo, however, did not forget about hang gliding. After World War II, Dr. Rogallo and his wife Gertrude developed a kite-like wing. Some adventurous water-skiers in Australia used the Rogallo wing to create a new sport. The skiers tied one end of a towrope to the end of a motorboat. They held on to the other end of the rope. As the motorboat gained speed in the water, the skiers, wearing the Rogallo wing, rose into the air, leaving their skis on the water. Once they reached a certain height, they would let go of the towrope. Then they would use the wing to glide back to Earth.

Two of these skiers, Bill Moyes and Bill Bennett, came to the United States in the 1960s. They demonstrated their daring sport to thrilled crowds. American Richard Miller, inspired by Moyes and Bennett, designed his own wing. This wing was bigger than the Rogallo wing. Miller made a foot launch in California in 1965. A foot launch is when a pilot runs several steps with his or her glider, then uses the wind

For many years after airplanes were invented, the future of hang gliding seemed cloudy.

to take off. Onlookers remarked how Miller guided his craft by hanging from a frame. The term *hang gliding* began to catch on.

In the 1970s, hang gliding started to become popular. Small companies that built hang gliders sprouted up in the United States. Hang gliding spread to Europe a few years later. There are now hang glider pilots all over the world. The Hang Gliding and Paragliding Commission is an international group in charge of all hang gliding organizations. The commission keeps track of world hang gliding records. It also directs international competitions.

Hang gliding attracts people from many places and all walks of life. The sport isn't just for guys, either. About 15 percent of pilots are women. All glider pilots love the thrill of leaving solid ground. They long to soar through the skies. The element of danger is also attractive. They know that they have to work with the winds and weather conditions to stay aloft. Pilots know that a lapse in concentration could cost them dearly. This thrill keeps them launching over and over again.

It doesn't take long to learn the basics of gliding—especially when you have good weather and a great teacher. It is hard, however, to really master the sport.

Thanks to hang gliding, soaring over Earth is no longer just for the birds.

If you want to fly with the grace and precision of birds, you have to keep returning to the skies.

CHAPTER TWO

FLY RIGHT

WHICH KIND OF WING?

Hang gliding doesn't require a lot of expensive gear. In fact, it may be the cheapest way you can fly! Certainly, the most necessary piece of equipment is the glider. The most common kind is called a flex-wing. It earned this name because it's somewhat flexible. Flex-wings are usually made from an aluminum frame, steel cables, and a polyester sail. Curved aluminum rods, called battens, are inserted into the sail. These battens help give the wing the right shape. Battens work kind of like tent poles. Before you set up a tent, it's just a flat, folded sheet. Once you insert the poles, however, the tent takes shape and snaps into place.

Not all pilots use flex-wing gliders. Some use what are called rigid-wings. Rigid-wings are made from stiffer material than polyester, such as fiberglass.

Hang glider pilots can find great wind conditions all over the world. This pilot is soaring over Mt. Haleakala, in Hawaii.

Rigid-wings are heavier than flex-wings. They also tend to outperform flex-wings. Because of this, there are separate classes for flex-wings and rigid-wings in competitions.

STRAPPING IN

Pilots connect to their wings with hang straps. They also attach harnesses, made of strong webbing, to their glider's frames. This harness looks like a hammock. It helps a pilot rest comfortably on long flights. After all, the best flights can turn into daylong adventures. Glider harnesses help preserve pilots' energy, keeping them from getting exhausted.

Pilots wear helmets and parachutes in order to land safely. Many use special instruments such as variometers and altimeters. Variometers measure the speed in which pilots are lifting or sinking. Altimeters measure how high the pilots are flying. If the pilots reach extremely high altitudes, they may need to breathe through an oxygen mask. Without using these masks, pilots can get sick. If this happens, their judgment may be impaired. Often, pilots will take two-way radios with them. They use these to communicate

Always make sure you're accompanied by an instructor when you begin hang gliding. Your first flight is no time to try to wing it.

with other hang glider pilots, or with spectators on the ground.

GIVE ME A LIFT

Although pilots soar like birds, they do not have to flap their wings. However, they must learn to master a few techniques: launching, controlling the glider, and landing. This sounds simple—yet it requires hours of flying practice to perfect these skills.

Many hang gliders call their sport a "chess game with nature." It's an interesting observation. Pilots must make dozens of careful decisions over the

course of a single flight. They must be patient before making any sudden moves. Of course, if you make a wrong move in a chess game, you only lose a game piece. If you make careless judgements or get impatient while hang gliding, you could lose a lot more!

Any pilot will say that hang gliding is definitely an *X-treme* sport. While pilots may not need huge amounts of strength to hang glide, they do need maturity. Maturity prevents pilots from making reckless decisions. Pilots need strong reflexes to react quickly in pressure-packed moments. They also need good balance to avoid sharp, sudden dives. To keep from diving, gliders must find pockets of lift. Lift is air that moves upward. Lift carries pilots higher and allows them to stay aloft longer.

RIDGE LIFT AND THERMALS

There are two major ways pilots make their gliders rise: Riding ridge lift and riding thermals. Ridge lift is air that strikes an obstacle, such as a mountain ridge. After this air hits an obstacle, it deflects upward. Pilots seek out lift bands to aid their ascent. These lift bands form on the windy side of ridges.

Hang gliding even makes the skies friendly for man's best friend!

Thermals are bubbles or columns of warm air. Thermal lift occurs when the sun heats up the ground. This heat transfers to the surrounding air. As this air heats up, it rises. A pilot catches a thermal by circling the warm air. That's not as easy as it sounds. Not only are thermals invisible, they also move when pushed by strong winds. Pilots have to practice thermaling to learn how to locate and take advantage of air currents. It's well worth the effort, though. Once a pilot locates a great thermal, the hot air can push him or her upward at a staggering rate of 1,500 feet (.48 kilometers) per minute. Such thermals can send you past the clouds—up to 20,000 feet (6.1 km) above the ground!

SITE SPECIFIC

Pilots often begin flights from sand dunes, hillsides, or the slopes of mountains. They use a foot launch from these types of flying sites. This is easier to do when the winds are light. The stronger the wind, the more skill the pilot will need to launch.

Hang glider pilots don't have to launch from a mountainous area. They can launch from areas that are

A hillside like this is a perfect place to execute a smooth foot launch.

perfectly flat. In fact, one pilot, who launched in the flattest part of southern Texas, set a world record. How can a pilot launch without jumping from the slope of a hill for takeoff? Pilots on flat ground are towed into the air by a vehicle driving along the ground, or by an ultralight aircraft. When gliders get high enough, they detach from the tow vehicle.

After a successful launch, pilots need to decide where to go. They shift their bodies to steer and guide their gliders. To turn the glider, a pilot shifts to the right or to the left. To increase the speed of gliders, pilots shift their body weight forward. To slow down, pilots just shift their weight backward.

When they're not changing their altitude, pilots try to keep their gliders level with the ground. Of course, nature may have other ideas! Sometimes, heavy, cold air will jolt a hang glider. When this happens, the glider's nose goes from a level position into a nosedive. This is called "going over the falls." If a pilot tilts and dives too severely, he or she will slam into the glider's underside. The impact can destroy the glider instantly. When this happens, the pilot must detach from the glider and use an emergency parachute that he or she wears. If the nosedive isn't so severe, experienced pilots can shift their weight forward. A few fancy maneuvers can help gain back airspeed and control.

Once weariness sets in, or the lifts die down, pilots have to land. One technique that helps pilots land safely and softly is flaring. Flaring means to raise the glider's nose smoothly just as you're about to land. Flaring helps make the glider level. Pilots who time their flares well are rewarded with gentle landings.

X-treme pilots can't have any hang-ups, or fears, of great heights.

CHAPTER THREE

WINGING IT

How do pilots go from flying for fun to flying in competitions? It takes a lot of practice. During a hang gliding contest, pilots strive to reach a variety of difficult goals. During the earliest competitions, pilots had modest goals. They simply tried to stay airborne, perform a few maneuvers, and land gracefully. Over the years, wing manufacturers kept improving the quality of the gliders. Pilots also gained more skills. Thanks to these improvements, pilots could soon embrace bigger and more dangerous goals. Hang gliding competitions now include timed races of more than 100 miles (161 km). Pilots also can compete in distance and endurance events.

Hang gliding competitions take place all across the world. Pilots come from dozens of nations to compete. The Hang Gliding and Paragliding Commission oversees these extraordinary events.

As hang gliding enthusiasts get more and more skilled at piloting, many choose to enter competitions.

LIKE FATHER, LIKE SON

Australian Bill Moyes, as you know, helped create the sport of hang gliding. Bill was well-known for his daring flights. He even launched from the south rim of the Grand Canyon. Bill's son, Steve, was awed by his father's adventures. Steve followed Bill's flight path, becoming a world-champion hang gliding pilot.

Who are some of the world's top pilots? A Czech named Tomas Suchanek would have to qualify. He's won three world championships during his career! An Australian pilot, Manfred Ruhmer, won second place in the 1995 Hang Gliding World Championship. His score was just behind Suchanek's. In 2001, Ruhmer set a world record for distance. He flew 432 miles (695.2 km) at the World Record Encampment in Zapata, Texas.

American pilots have made their mark as well. Kari Castle is a top female hang glider. Like Manfred Ruhmer, Castle also dazzled fellow pilots at the World Record Encampment. Castle had injured her knee in a 1999 launching accident. Yet she made a huge comeback in 2001. She flew 250 miles (402.3 km)—a record for a female pilot!

Just because gliding lets you soar like a bird doesn't mean you'll always land like one. This pilot took a nasty spill on his return approach to solid ground.

COMPETITION TIME

Many hang gliding competitions last an entire week. Each morning, pilots have to compete at a different task. They earn points based on how quickly, and how well, they complete it. They can earn up to 1,000 points every day. At the end of the meet, the pilots with the best scores win prizes.

One major meet that serious pilots like to tackle is the Sandia Classic. This event is held under the stunning backdrop of New Mexico's 10,000-foot (3.1-km) Sandia Peak. Competitors race against the clock to complete the course in the quickest time, soaring and swooping at blazing speeds.

Pilots face stiff winds and a difficult course at Sandia. Only experts are allowed to tackle it. Pilots must wait for a launch window. That's when wind conditions are perfect for gliding. A perfect launch window doesn't stay open for long. When pilots get one, they must leap into action. They photograph the spot from where they launch. They must also take snapshots of major turning points, as well as their landing spot. This evidence proves they took the proper course.

GAGGLES, BUT NOT OF GEESE

Geese that fly together are called a gaggle. This word is also used for a group of hang gliding pilots who fly together. Pilots often fly in gaggles during competitions. Flying together helps them spot when other gliders have found some lift. They all head to that area to try to share the lift. They also watch for when other pilots hit an area of sink. Sink is caused when wind currents blow downward. Hitting sink means that a glider is going to be pushed lower. Like geese, gaggles of hang gliders sometimes call to each other during flights. They use their radios to report when they've found a thermal or hit sink.

Sometimes, competitors wind up facing hazards other than sinks, or drops in flying height, and nose-dives. A few pilots have had very close encounters with real birds. Since birds are the true experts at finding lift, many pilots try to follow their lead. If they see a bird ascending, the pilots try to tag along. Sometimes, though, the bird isn't too happy with being tailed. Pilots have reported hawks and falcons diving at them, slashing their sails with razor-sharp talons.

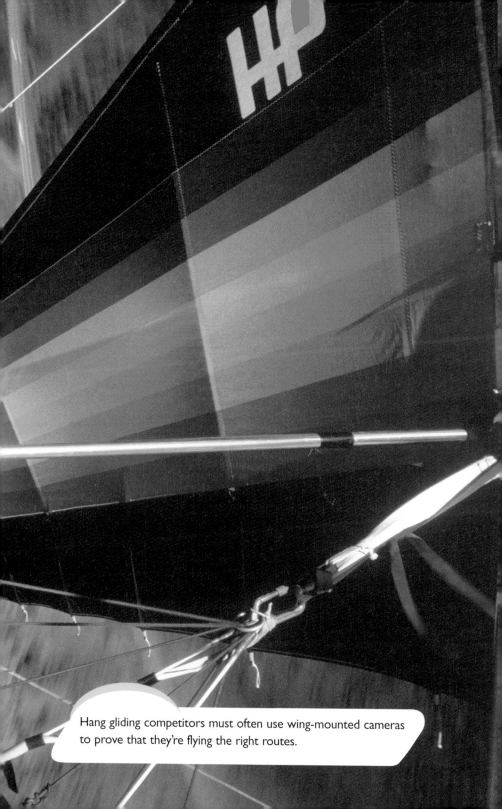

Hang gliding competitors must often use wing-mounted cameras to prove that they're flying the right routes.

TEAMING UP

Hang glider pilots sometimes compete as members of teams. Teams are often made up of groups of pilots who come from the same country. Each team is made up of five to eight pilots. Each day, all of the pilots compete in the same events. The top three scores are counted each day. Once the meet is over, the team with the highest score wins.

For a long time, the British team was the top international team. It performed well because the pilots trained in England's extreme weather conditions. The team stayed at the top of worldwide competition for nearly fifteen years.

X-FACTOR

In 1993, the U.S. hang gliding team made its mark. It shocked the British team by winning the world title.

Tired of hanging around the house all day? Ask your parents if you can hang in the skies instead.

CHAPTER FOUR

SKY HIGH

Do you think you're ready to hang with the birds? Let's see if you qualify. To begin hang gliding lessons, you have to be at least twelve years old. You must also weigh at least 85 pounds (38.6 kilograms). You should take your lessons from a certified instructor. The United States Hang Gliding Association (USHGA) can provide you with a list of certified instructors.

The USHGA has a licensing program for people who want to learn to be hang glider pilots. This program is similar to the program that airplane pilots have to complete. The licensing program is made up of pilot proficiency ratings. These ratings range from Beginner through Master. The higher your rating, the more flying skills you possess.

Although hot air pushes hang gliders higher, the air actually becomes colder as they ascend. The temperature drops 4 °Fahrenheit (2.2 °Celsius) for each 1,000 feet (304.8 meters) climbed.

Here are some recommended guidelines for a Beginner-rated pilot:

- Fly only under the guidance of an instructor;
- Fly only from hills under 100 feet (38.5 m) in height;
- Fly only in mild winds.

Hang gliding pilots aren't restricted by law in the ways that airplane pilots are. However, most flying sites in the United States require that you show your USHGA pilot rating before any launch. Each flying site is rated. This way, pilots can ensure their skill levels are equal to the level of difficulty of the site.

FREQUENT FLYERS

Just how long will it take before you are soaring through the sky? That depends on your natural skill and a little luck. If you've got good weather and manageable terrain, your training may go more smoothly. You'll probably need between five and ten lessons to reach the first USHGA pilot rating of Beginner. This can take from three to six months to complete. It takes about the same amount of lessons and months to reach the second USHGA rating of Novice.

Some fliers have a busier schedule than others. This pilot in Switzerland soared over towns dressed as Santa Claus to deliver gifts to lucky kids!

SOARING COSTS

Here's a price range of the gear you will need to go on solo
hang gliding adventures.

Training (through Novice level):	$600	$1200
Training glider (used):	$400	$1500
Training glider (new):	$2500	$3500
Harness (new):	$200	$700
Parachute (new):	$450	$550
Helmet (new):	$80	$300

Feeling a bit of sticker shock? Before you take out your
wallet, remember: You don't have to get all this equipment
when you start. Most schools include training equipment
in the cost of your lessons.

In early lessons, you may learn by using towing
training. You and your instructor will be pulled into the
air on a two-place glider. Once you get high enough,
the instructor will release the towline. Then he or she
will begin teaching you how to control the glider by
shifting your weight. Wheels attached to the glider will
help ease your landing. After you've logged many practice flights, you'll get to fly solo.

Before you're allowed to fly the skies solo, an instructor will need to tag along with you.

Your first landings may be pretty awkward. The wind might flip you as you try to flare. You may take a tumble or two as you're learning the techniques. Be patient, though, and don't get discouraged. Eventually, you will learn to land on your feet.

After you complete your primary training, you'll get to start spreading your wings. The instructor will let you launch from higher altitudes. You'll be taking off anywhere from a few hundred, to several thousand, feet. In no time at all, you'll have your head above the clouds, and a beautiful, birds-eye view of Earth.

Seize one of life's great freedoms—go hang gliding!

NEW WORDS

altimeters instruments that measure height above ground or sea level

Beginner the first level of pilot rating as determined by the USHGA

dive to fly downward at a sharp angle

flaring a landing technique that makes the glider parallel with the ground

gaggle the name given to a group of geese, as well as a group of hang glider pilots

glide to move through the air in a forward and downward direction

lift upwardly moving air used by pilots to gain altitude

Novice the second level of pilot rating as determined by the USHGA; required for solo flights

NEW WORDS

proficiency advancement or progress

ridge lift air that hits an object and then moves upward along a hill or ridge

Rogallo wing an early type of hang glider

sink wind currents that move downward and cause gliders to lose altitude

terrain physical features of land

thermal a column or bubble of warm, rising air

two-place glider a glider designed to be flown by two people

variometers instruments that measure vertical speed

FOR FURTHER READING

Italia, Bob. *Hang Gliding: Action Sports*. Edina, MN: ABDO Publishing Company, 1994.

Perry, Phyllis Jean. *Soaring*. Danbury, CT: Franklin Watts, 1997.

Radlauer, Ed. *Some Basics About Hang Gliding*. Chicago, IL: Children's Press, 1979.

Will-Harris, Toni. *Hang Gliding and Parasailing*. Mankato, MN: Capstone Press, 1992.

RESOURCES

Web Sites

United States Hang Gliding Association, Inc.

www.ushga.org

Visit this site to find out more information about certified hang gliding schools. The site also provides links to the USHGA's monthly magazine, *Hang Gliding*.

The World Air Sports Federation

www.fai.org

This is the official Web site for the World Air Sports Federation. This organization sets rules and keeps records for all kinds of air sports, including hang gliding. Visit this site to learn the results of the latest hang gliding competitions.

RESOURCES

Airsports Net

www.usairnet.com

This Web site offers information about various air sports, including hang gliding. Check out its bulletin boards where you can learn more about big events and communicate with other hang gliding enthusiasts.

INDEX

INDEX

About the Author

Heidi Zeigler grew up in Texas, not far from the spot where several hang gliding records have been set. She currently lives and works in Boulder, Colorado, where she writes poetry and non-fiction literature. Heidi teaches at Front Range Community College in Colorado, as a professor of English.